First World War
and Army of Occupation
War Diary
France, Belgium and Germany

60 DIVISION
Headquarters, Branches and Services
Royal Army Veterinary Corps
Assistant Director Veterinary Services
21 June 1916 - 30 November 1916

WO95/3026/11

The Naval & Military Press Ltd
www.nmarchive.com
Published in association with The National Archives

Published by

The Naval & Military Press Ltd

Unit 10 Ridgewood Industrial Park,

Uckfield, East Sussex,

TN22 5QE England

Tel: +44 (0) 1825 749494

www.naval-military-press.com

www.nmarchive.com

This diary has been reprinted in facsimile from the original. Any imperfections are inevitably reproduced and the quality may fall short of modern type and cartographic standards.

© **Crown Copyright**
Images reproduced by permission of The National Archives, London, England, 2015.

Contents

Document type	Place/Title	Date From	Date To
Heading	WO95/3026/11		
Heading	60th Division Asst Dir. Vety Services Jun-Nov 1916		
Heading	War Diary of A.D.V.S 60th Division		
War Diary	Southampton	21/06/1916	25/06/1916
War Diary	Havre	26/06/1916	28/06/1916
War Diary	Villers Chatel	29/06/1916	30/06/1916
War Diary	Savy And Camblain L'Abbe	30/06/1916	30/06/1916
Heading	War Diary of A.D.V.S 60th Division		
War Diary	Penin Chelers Bethonsart	01/07/1916	01/07/1916
War Diary	Ecoivres Savy Villers Chatel	02/07/1916	02/07/1916
War Diary	Mingoval Penin	03/07/1916	03/07/1916
War Diary	St Michel Etrun	04/07/1916	04/07/1916
War Diary	Bethonsart Hermaville	05/07/1916	05/07/1916
War Diary	St Pol and Ecoivres	06/07/1916	06/07/1916
War Diary	Gouy-En-Ternois Pt Houvin Maizaires Maroeuil	07/07/1916	07/07/1916
War Diary	Hermaville Tingues Bethonsart	08/07/1916	08/07/1916
War Diary	Acq Chelers Villers Chatel	09/07/1916	09/07/1916
War Diary	Hermaville Aubigny	10/07/1916	10/07/1916
War Diary	Mingoval Cambligneul	11/07/1916	11/07/1916
War Diary	Bethonsart Mt St Eloy Ecoivres Etrun	12/07/1916	12/07/1916
War Diary	Villers Chatel Ecoivres	13/07/1916	13/07/1916
War Diary	Hermaville	14/07/1916	14/07/1916
War Diary	Haute-Avesnes Acq	15/07/1916	15/07/1916
War Diary	Berles	16/07/1916	16/07/1916
War Diary	Amiens Acq Etrun	17/07/1916	17/07/1916
War Diary	Berles Aubigny	18/07/1916	18/07/1916
War Diary	Freyin Capglle Acq	19/07/1916	19/07/1916
War Diary	Larasset Ecoivres Aubigny	20/07/1916	20/07/1916
War Diary	Acq Haute-Avesnes Habarcq	21/07/1916	21/07/1916
War Diary	Ecoivres Acq Divisional Area & Aubigny	22/07/1916	22/07/1916
War Diary	Sectors Louez Aubigny	23/07/1916	23/07/1916
War Diary	Mt St Eloy Maroeuil	24/07/1916	24/07/1916
War Diary	Habarcq Berles Aubigny	25/07/1916	25/07/1916
War Diary	Savy Frevin Capelle	26/07/1916	26/07/1916
War Diary	Acq Haute-Avesnes	27/07/1916	27/07/1916
War Diary	Hermaville Louez Aubigny	28/07/1916	28/07/1916
War Diary	Ecoivres Mt St Eloy Maroeuil Anzin	29/07/1916	29/07/1916
War Diary	Aubigny	30/07/1916	30/07/1916
War Diary	Aubigny Habarcq	31/07/1916	31/07/1916
Heading	A.D.V.S. 60th Division War Diary August 1916 Vol III		
War Diary	Hermaville	01/08/1916	31/08/1916
Heading	War Diary September 1916 Vol 4		
War Diary	Hermaville	03/09/1916	30/09/1916
Heading	War Diary of A.D.V.S. 60th Division October 1916 Vol 5		
War Diary	Hermaville	02/10/1916	25/10/1916
War Diary	Houvin-Houvigneul	26/10/1916	27/10/1916
War Diary	Frohen-Le-Grand	28/10/1916	28/10/1916
War Diary	Bernaville	29/10/1916	31/10/1916
Heading	War Diary November 1916 Vol 6		

War Diary	Bernaville	01/11/1916	03/11/1916
War Diary	Ailly Le Haut Clocher	07/11/1916	20/11/1916
War Diary	Longpre	24/11/1916	24/11/1916
War Diary	Marseilles	26/11/1916	30/11/1916

WO 95/3026/1"

60TH DIVISION

ASST DIR. VETY SERVICES
JUN-NOV 1916

War Diary of

**A.D.V.S.
60TH DIVISION.**

June 1916.

Vol 1

Army Form C. 2118.

WAR DIARY
or
INTELLIGENCE SUMMARY.

(Erase heading not required.)

June 1916

Instructions regarding War Diaries and Intelligence Summaries are contained in F. S. Regs., Part II. and the Staff Manual respectively. Title pages will be prepared in manuscript.

Place	Date	Hour	Summary of Events and Information	Remarks and references to Appendices
Southampton	21.6.16		Left SUTTON VENY JUNE 20th 1916 for SOUTHAMPTON	
"	22.6.16		Remained at DOCKS re embarkation of animals until evening of 25th.	
"	23.6.16		Very few animals were taken away by the Veterinary Inspectors. Embarkation officers stated that our	
"	24.6.16		animals were in better condition than most Divisions which they had seen, and that fewer animals were	
"	25.6.16		taken out (for sickness and unfitness) as compared to other DIVISIONS.	
HAVRE	26.6.16		Arrived HAVRE 4 p.m.	
"	27.6.16		Remained with D.A.C. HAVRE until evening of 28th BLEVILLE CAMP, HAVRE, weather very wet. Camp a mass of mud. Animals D.A.C. suffered a good deal. On 26th hay ration very small	
"	28.6.16		1. train HAVRE to ST POL.	
VILLERS CHATEL	29.6.16		Arrived DIVISIONAL HEADQUARTERS.	
SAVY AND CAMBLAIN L'ABBE	30.6.16		Visited Mobile Veterinary Section, Signal Coy. VILLERS CHATEL and Divisional Train SAVY. H.Q Coy " A.D.V.S. 2nd DIVISION, CAMBLAIN L'ABBE. Applied for FLOAT to move sick horses.	

H H Cameron
A.D.V.S.
60TH DIVISION.

Secret

July 1916.

Vol II

War Diary of.

A.D.V.S.
60TH DIVISION.

WAR DIARY or INTELLIGENCE SUMMARY

Army Form C. 2118.

(Erase heading not required.)

July 1916

Instructions regarding War Diaries and Intelligence Summaries are contained in F.S. Regs., Part II. and the Staff Manual respectively. Title pages will be prepared in manuscript.

Place	Date	Hour	Summary of Events and Information	Remarks and references to Appendices
PENIN, CHELERS BETHONSART	1.7.16		Visited Field Coys R.E. + Field Ambulances, PENIN, CHELERS and 302nd Brigade R.F.A. BETHONSART.	
ECOIVRES. SAVY. VILLERS CHATEL	2.7.16		300th Brigade RFA ECOIVRES and DIVISIONAL TRAIN. SAVY. Mobile Veterinary Section. VILLERS CHATEL.	
MINGOVAL PENIN.	3.7.16		Visited 303rd Brigade R.F.A. MINGOVAL + 180th Infantry Bde. PENIN.	
ST MICHEL. ETRUN.	4.7.16		No sick horses left with MAIRE. Visited 181st Infantry Brigade ETRUN.	
BETHONSART HERMAVILLE	6.7.16		Visited A.D.V.S. 51st DIVISION. 301st Brigade R.F.A. BETHONSART. Office work.	
ST POL AND ECOIVRES.	6.7.16		D.D.V.S. IIIRD ARMY. 6TH FIELD AMBULANCE, ECOIVRES.	
GOUY-EN-TERROIS PT HOUVIN MAIZAINES MARCEUIL	7.7.16		{ Re sick horses left in field, and open joint case R.E. PT HOUVIN 5TH FIELD AMBULANCE Gouy-en-Terrois 180TH Inf Brigade. MARCEUIL. Quantities of wire, jagged tin etc. are noticed in horse lines of many units.	
HERMAVILLE TINGUES BETHONSART	8.7.16		Visited A.D.V.S. 51ST DIVISION. HERMAVILLE, Divisional Train, TINGUES 3 + 4 Coys. 302nd Brigade R.F.A. BETHONSART.	
ACQ CHELERS VILLERS CHATEL	9.7.16		181st Inf Brigade ACQ. Field Ambulances CHELERS. Mobile Veterinary Section. VILLERS CHATEL. Office work.	
HERMAVILLE AUBIGNY	10.7.16		Office work. Visited A.D.V.S. 51ST DIVISION re suggested stabling to be taken over by M.V.S. { Large number of "PICKED UP NAIL" cases amongst animals at this period. D.D.V.S. III ARMY Visited Mobile Veterinary Section.	
MINGOVAL CAMBLIGNEUIL	11.7.16		5TH Field Ambulance. DIVISIONAL AMM. COLUMN inspected. Office work	
BETHONSART Mt ST ELOY ECOIVRES. ETRUN.	12.7.16		301ST Brigade BETHONSART. Field Coys R.E. Mt. St Eloy, Ecoivres, Etrun.	

A.D.V.S.
60TH DIVISION.

July 1916 (Continued)

WAR DIARY or INTELLIGENCE SUMMARY

Army Form C. 2118.

Place	Date	Hour	Summary of Events and Information	Remarks and references to Appendices
VILLERS CHATEL ECOIVRES.	13.7.16		Mobile Veterinary Section. 179th Infantry Brigade, ECOIVRES. Office work.	
HERMAVILLE.	14.7.16		Move of Divisional Headquarters to HERMAVILLE. Office work.	
HAUTE-AVESNES. ACQ. BERLES.	15.7.16		303rd Brigade R.F.A. ACQ. Divisional Train. HAUTE-AVESNES.	
BERLES.	16.7.16		Visited Dog at BERLES, suspected of RABIES, on instructions of D.D.V.S. IIIrd ARMY. that's Veterinary BERLES. Picked up Nail cases still numerous, and quantities of wire, to place etc which might injure horses are to be found on many farm lands.	
AMIENS. ACQ 17.7.16 ETRUN.	17.7.16		Amiens. purchased 5 small Anvils, as some of our anvils too heavy. Sent 1 to M.V.S., 1 Divnl H.Q. and 1 each Infantry Brigade. Visited 179th Brigade ETRUN, 300th Brigade, R.F.A. ACQ.	
BERLES. AUBIGNY	18.7.16		Visited dog (Suspected Rabies). Dog had bitten several men, and had been under my observation - was not affected with Rabies. Visited 21st Res. Park, BERLES, and Yorkshire Hussars, BERLES. Office.	
FREVIN CAPELLE ACQ.	19.7.16		Visited D.A.C. FREVIN CAPELLE, 302nd BRIGADE R.F.A. ACQ. In the various billeting centres there quantities of Carpenter's nails in places on the ground. These are often picked up by the feet of horses. I am arranging for these nails to be collected as most serious injuries to the feet of several horses have occurred. Jagged pieces of tin, pieces of wire etc, also collected.	
LARASSET ECOIVRES AUBIGNY	20.7.16		Visited 301st Brigade R.F.A. LARASSET, 180th Infantry Brigade ECOIVRES, 4th Field Ambulance ECOIVRES. and animals of 17th Corps H.Q. AUBIGNY.	
HAUTE AVESNES BERLES	21.7.16		Visited 300th Brigade R.F.A. ACQ. Divisional Train and Field Ambulances. HAUTE AVESNES, 17th Corps H.A. HABARCQ. Office work.	

A.D.V.S.
60TH DIVISION.

Army Form C. 2118.

July 1916 (Continued)

WAR DIARY
or
INTELLIGENCE SUMMARY.
(Erase heading not required.)

Instructions regarding War Diaries and Intelligence Summaries are contained in F.S. Regs., Part II. and the Staff Manual respectively. Title pages will be prepared in manuscript.

Place	Date	Hour	Summary of Events and Information	Remarks and references to Appendices
ECOIVRES, ACQ DIVISIONAL AREA & AUBIGNY.	22.7.16		13th Battalion. ECOIVRES. 181st Infantry Brigade. ACQ. Accompanied D.A.Q.M.G. 17th Corps around horse lines of Divisional Area. Mobile Veterinary Section. AUBIGNY.	
SECTORS LOUEZ AUBIGNY.	23.7.16		Pioneer Battalion. LOUEZ. Machine Gun Companies. Mobile Veterinary Section. AUBIGNY. Office.	
MT ST ELOY MARŒUIL	24.7.16		303rd Brigade RFA and No 3 Coy A.S.C. ACQ. Field Cos RE. MARŒUIL & MT ST ELOY.	
HABARCQ BERLES AUBIGNY.	25.7.16		17th Corps H.A. HABARCQ. Yorks Hussars and Hants Yeomanry. BERLES. 21st Res Park. BERLES. Mobile Veterinary Section. AUBIGNY. Office. Wire de l'astillel hired in loose lines of unit. Order published re P.U.N. cases.	
SAVY FREVIN CAPELLE	26.7.16		Visited A.D.V.S. Indian Cavalry Division. SAVY. D.A.C. FREVIN CAPELLE.	
ACQ HAUTE-AVESNES	27.7.16		300th 303rd Brigade. ACQ. 5th Y&L Field Ambulances and H.Q. Coy A.S.C. HAUTE AVESNES.	
HERMAVILLE LOUEZ AUBIGNY.	28.7.16		Signal Coy R.E., Pioneer Battalion. LOUEZ. Mobile Veterinary Section. AUBIGNY. Office. Wire de la stilletis still prevalent in horse lines of units. Order published re P.U.N. cases still prevalent. Plant arrived from R.S.P.C.A. after several applications.	
ECOIVRES MT ST ELOY MARŒUIL ANZIN	29.7.16		179th Infantry Brigade ECOIVRES. 180th Infantry Brigade. MT ST ELOY. Field Cos RE. ANZIN, MARŒUIL. Office. This is evidently a "Tetanus district". Indented for Anti-Tetanin.	
AUBIGNY	30.7.16		Remounts arrived AUBIGNY Station (a good lot). Mobile Veterinary Section. AUBIGNY. Mallein Testing Signal Coy R.E. (No reactors)	
AUBIGNY HABARCQ	31.7.16		Remounts arrived AUBIGNY Station. Mobile Veterinary Section. AUBIGNY. 17th Corps H.A. HABARCQ. Office work	

A.D.V.S.
60TH DIVISION.

A.D.V.S.
60TH DIVISION.

Vol III

War Diary
August 1916.

Army Form C. 2118.

August 1916

WAR DIARY
or
INTELLIGENCE SUMMARY.
(Erase heading not required.)

Instructions regarding War Diaries and Intelligence Summaries are contained in F. S. Regs., Part II. and the Staff Manual respectively. Title pages will be prepared in manuscript.

Place	Date	Hour	Summary of Events and Information	Remarks and references to Appendices
HERMAVILLE	1.8.16		MALLEIN TESTING D.H.Q. (No re-actors) Office work. "Picked up nail" cases decreasing but wire & broken tins still to be found in several Horse lines. Visited Mobile Veterinary Section AUBIGNY.	
"	2.8.16		No 11. Sergt Freett A.V.C. found incapable of performing duties of Sergeant A.V.C. and instruction of D.D.V.S. IIIrd ARMY. Mallening D.H.Q. Signal Coy RE & FrR R.A. & R.E. Visited D.A.C. FREVIN CAPELLE and evacuated to BASE. (Wounds on feet and legs seem to heal slowly, laceration seen cuts in and bad)	
"	3.8.16		Visited 301st Brigade R.F.A. LARASSET. Divisional Train HAUTE AVESNES, Mobile Veterinary Section. AUBIGNY. No re-action from Mallein Testing previous day	
"	4.8.16		No 207 Sergt Martin A.V.C. Evacuated to ENGLAND suffering from Shell shock. Visited 303rd Brigade A.C.Q. and 179th Inf Bde ECOIVRES. Still too much wire in and near lines, also pieces of iron which might injure horses – on feet and legs.	
"	5.8.16		Visited 180th Infantry Bde, Mt ST ELOY. 302ND Brigade A.C.Q. Field Coys R.E. ANZIN, Mt ST ELOY ECURIE. All animals of DIVISION have been "malleined" – no re-actions. But as they were all tested hypodermically about two months ago, I did not expect to get re-actions, especially when the small dose of the Ophtalmic Mallein is considered.	

M. Meach
Lt Col.
A.D.V.S.
60TH DIVISION.

August 1916 (Continued)

WAR DIARY or INTELLIGENCE SUMMARY.
Army Form C. 2118.

(Erase heading not required.)

Instructions regarding War Diaries and Intelligence Summaries are contained in F. S. Regs., Part II. and the Staff Manual respectively. Title pages will be prepared in manuscript.

Place	Date	Hour	Summary of Events and Information	Remarks and references to Appendices
HERMAVILLE	6.8.16		Visited 300TH & 303rd Brigade R.F.A. ACQ. 181st Infantry Brigade ACQ. Mobile Veterinary Section AUBIGNY. Reported to C.R.A. re too much wire and old tins in R.F.A. Lines ACQ. in some cases showing great carelessness.	
"	7.8.16		Visited 301ST Brigade LARASSET. 17TH Corps. H.A. HABARCQ. M.A. have too many sick horses. Reported to D.D.R. Office work.	
"	8.8.16		D.A.C. FREVIN CAPELLE. 181st Inf Bde ACQ. M.V.S. AUBIGNY. Pack horses and mules Infantry are not used. About 15 Pack animals per Brigade do no work as they are too small for draught. Reported D.D.R. but he says, after inspecting, that at present L.D. horses are not available.	
"	9.8.16		Remounts with D.D.R. DOUSSANS. Office. Signal Coy R.E.	
"	10.8.16		302nd Brigade R.F.A. ACQ. 179TH & 180TH Infantry Brigades ECOIVRES & MISTELOY. M.V.S. AUBIGNY	
"	11.8.16		20T Battalion Machine Gun Companies ECOIVRES & ETRUN. 5 & 6T Field Ambulance HAUTE AVESNES. H.T. Field Ambulance, ECOIVRES. Office. Machine Gun Coys - wire, iron etc laying about. Shoeing Machine Gun Coys, bad. Only 1 Shoeing Smith per Company. Arranged for I.S.S. to be lent to each Company from Brigade, and arranged for training of men.	
"	12.8.16		Visited D.A.C. FREVIN CAPELLE & M.V.S. AUBIGNY. Office work. There are too many kicks and injuries in D.A.C. Have gone into matter with C.R.A. who is arranging for greater care re these animals, and more supervision by officers.	

A.D.V.S.
60TH DIVISION.

Army Form C. 2118.

WAR DIARY
or
INTELLIGENCE SUMMARY.
(Erase heading not required.)

August 1916
(Contd)

Place	Date	Hour	Summary of Events and Information	Remarks and references to Appendices
HERMAVILLE	13.8.16		Inspected stables at CAPELLE FERMONT labelled "GLANDERS & MANGE". Visited 303rd Brigade ACQ. Mobile Veterinary Section AUBIGNY.	
"	14.8.16		D.A.C. FREVIN CAPELLE. 1/6th FIELD Coy R.E. MARŒUIL. 17th Corps H.A. HABARCQ. Pioneer Battalion LOUEZ. Horse lines of Pioneer Battalion well kept. H.A. have several serious cases. Too much wire about their lines.	
"	15.8.16		Divisional Train. HAUTE AVESNES. 4th Field Ambulance. No 3 Coy A.S.C. ECOIVRES + ACQ. Office work. 4th Field Ambulance lines not well kept. Too much wire and bits of iron about.	
"	16.8.16		M.V.S. AUBIGNY. Office work. Cept Hill severely injured through fall from horse. Animal took fright at tractor Engine.	
"	17.8.16		Remounts arrived AUBIGNY STATION. (72). Inspection with DDR of Pack Animals in 179th, 180th, 181st Inf Bdes. Remounts :- 9 R.A. in poor condition. It is sheer waste of money and time to keep in Depots at the base, such old and useless animals as these fourteen. 3 L.D. Mules - old and weak 2 L.D. horses - lame and weak - evacuated	
"	18.8.16		M.V.S. AUBIGNY. 302nd Brigade R.F.A. ACQ. 181st Infantry Brigade ACQ. Field Coys R.E. ANZIN, ETRUN, MARŒUIL. M.V.S. AUBIGNY. Office.	
"	19.8.16		Machine Gun Companies. Signal Coy R.E. Office. Machine Gun Companies keeping their lines rather better. Signal Coy lines well kept. Horses improving.	

A.D.V.S.
60TH DIVISION.

WAR DIARY or INTELLIGENCE SUMMARY

August 1916 (Contd)

Army Form C. 2118.

Place	Date	Hour	Summary of Events and Information	Remarks and references to Appendices
HERMAVILLE	20.8.16		D.A.C. FREVIN CAPELLE. A.C.Q. Oranged with Staff Captain 181st Infantry Brigade re winter standings and road. M.V.S. Aubigny. Office.	
	21.8.16		M/E Corps H.A. HABARCQ. 5th & 6th Field Ambulances. HAUTE AVESNES. H.Q. Coy A.S.C. HAUTE-AVESNES. Office	
	22.8.16		M.V.S. AUBIGNY re standings and Shelters for winter. Pioneer Battalion LOUEZ. Re winter standings Machine Gun Companies.	
	23.8.16		Office work. 302, 303 Brigade R.F.A. A.C.Q. C.H.Q. lines A.C.Q. are now kept better and more free from swine etc.	
	24.8.16		Mobile Veterinary Section. AUBIGNY. 179th Infantry Brigade ECOIVRES. 18th Battalion. Signal Coy R.E. Office.	
	25.8.16		D.A.C. FREVIN CAPELLE. 300TH Brigade A.C.Q. Most of horses and mules evacuated were issued as Remounts to this Division a few days before leaving Salisbury Plain and M.V.S. re animals for evacuation. There was no time to get these animals. Remounts to complete Division were applied for early in May, but in spite of several urgent representations, were not sent until second week in June. There is great danger from this practice of introducing contagious diseases, especially Mange, into a Division, as when a Division moves, Remounts cannot be isolated and watched.	
	26.7.16		M.V.S. AUBIGNY. 301st Brigade R.F.A. LARASSET. Conference on Winter Standings. Office work.	

G.M. Lane
A.D.V.S.
60TH DIVISION.

August 1916 (Contd.)

WAR DIARY
or
INTELLIGENCE SUMMARY.

Army Form C. 2118.

Place	Date	Hour	Summary of Events and Information	Remarks and references to Appendices
HERMAVILLE	27.8.16		Sorting surplus horses M.V.S. AUBIGNY. Very few fit to re-issue. In 302nd Brigade R.F.A. the isolation of 30 Remounts has not been properly carried out. In England almost every batch of Remounts arrived either with "MANGE", or developed this disease a week or two later. Only by strictly isolating all Remounts and Scrubbing them at least Twice with some dressing (such as arsenical Soap etc.), could this disease be prevented from spreading to the animals of this Division.	
	28.8.16		Visited L.N.Lancs Pioneer Battalion re H.D. horses. Office work.	
	29.8.16		Visited with Capt Hill A.V.C. L.N.Lancs Pioneer Battalion, LOUEZ, also Infantry Transport ETRUN and inspected horses 301st Brigade R.F.A. ACQ. M.V.S. AUBIGNY.	
	30.8.16		Sorting horses Mobile Veterinary Section AUBIGNY. Visited horse lines No.4. Field Ambulance re bad standings. This is not a matter of drainage, so called in Capt Tebbutt, Sanitary Officer, who is a Road Surveyor by Profession.	
	31.8.16		Sorting horses M.V.S. AUBIGNY. Visited Divisional Train, HAUTE AVESNES. Office	

F H Lever
A.D.V.S.
60TH DIVISION.

Vol 4

War Diary.
September 1916.

September 1916.

WAR DIARY
or
INTELLIGENCE SUMMARY.
(Erase heading not required.)

Army Form C. 2118.

Place	Date	Hour	Summary of Events and Information	Remarks and references to Appendices
HERMAVILLE	3.9.16		Surplus R.F.A. horses sent into M.V.S. These on the whole are a poor lot. Most are stiff and lame. Forwarded to Remount Report 74 — To Veterinary Hospital 14. Re-issued to units This Division 69. Total 157.	
"	4.9.16		Capt. J. Hill A.V.C. reports several cases lately of "Picked up Nails" by horses. These nails have in most cases been through fire — This is caused generally by throwing ashes out of a fire on to a road. (Iron with nails in) having been used as fuel.	
"	5.9.16		Issued 11 Riding horses out of Surplus R.F.A. Visited Divisional Train, HAUTE AVESNES. Exchanged 23 horses with Infantry Battalions.	
"	6.9.16		Inspected D.A.C. Some serious cases, chiefly kicks. Inspected water standings 5th & 6th FIELD AMBULANCE, arranged for Capt Tebbit, Sanitary Section, to do these.	
"	8.9.16		Inspected Machine Gun Contingents and reported to G.O.C. not enough men for mules. No forges. 179th M.G. Coy. 10 mules cannot be shod without stocks. Shoeing generally improving — was very bad. All mules require more exercise.	
"	9.9.16		Inspected R.F.A. ACQ. Lines fairly well kept, horses looking very well. 20 Remounts D 501 good, except one old gelding.	

A.D.V.S.
60TH DIVISION.

WAR DIARY or INTELLIGENCE SUMMARY

Army Form C. 2118.

September 1916 (Cont'd)

Place	Date	Hour	Summary of Events and Information	Remarks and references to Appendices
HERMAVILLE	10.9.16	-	D.A.C. No 1, 2 & 3 Section. Horses & mules generally looking well in condition. Shoeing fairly good. Selected four horses from No. 2 and One Mule from No. 1, and One mule and two horses No. 2 Section for evacuation.	
"	12.9.16		M.V.S. almost empty. 19. Surplus I.D.s absorbed.	
"	13.9.16		Tested riding horses D.A.C. D.D.R. 1st ARMY came over to arrange with D.A.Q.M.G and myself.	
"	15.9.16		D.D.V.S. FIRST ARMY came over. Visited PIONEER Battalion. General condition good. Except four mules evacuated. 14 Surplus horses from 303rd Brigade R.F.A.	
"	16.9.16		Mobile Veterinary Section, Sorting horses.	

H Leene Lt Col.
A.D.V.S.
60TH DIVISION.

Army Form C. 2118.

WAR DIARY
or
INTELLIGENCE SUMMARY
(Erase heading not required.)

Instructions regarding War Diaries and Intelligence Summaries are contained in F. S. Regs., Part II. and the Staff Manual respectively. Title Pages will be prepared in manuscript.

Place	Date	Hour	Summary of Events and Information	Remarks and references to Appendices
HERMAVILLE	17.9.16		303rd Brigade R.F.A. Also saw 3 horses LYMPHANGITIS cases – isolation Sheds.	
	18.9.16		D.D.V.S. and D.D.R. First Army called. Saw 7 R.F.A. Remounts at M.V.S. One lame and one unbroken.	
	19.9.16		Inspected 5 Units 179th Brigade. M.G. Coy improving. The 4 Infantry Battalions are looking after their horses well, and have done good work re hard standings and sheds.	
	21.9.16		Interviewed Capt BECKETT and Lieut JONES re Machine Gun Company 181st Brigade. Visited two horses (at CONTEVILLE) left by 20th Division. Both improving.	
	22.9.16		D.A.C. No 4 Section – 3 mules evacuated. No 2 Section 3 horses evacuated.	
	23.9.16		A & B. Batteries. 302 Brigade. A evacuated 4 Veterinary 1 Vice. B " 4 " "	

ATLeece Lt Col.
A.D.V.S.
60TH DIVISION.

Army Form C. 2118.

WAR DIARY
or
INTELLIGENCE SUMMARY

(Erase heading not required.)

Place	Date	Hour	Summary of Events and Information	Remarks and references to Appendices
HERMAVILLE	24.9.16	-	53 REMOUNTS arrived 5 P.m. inspected 130 mules D.A.C. MARŒUIL re Shoeing. About 30 mules feet far too long. Explained to Officers, N.C.O's and Farriers.	
"	25.9.16	-	Examining and issuing Remounts – a poor lot – Several very ill. Wrote D.D.R. saying at least eight cannot be issued – lame etc.	
"	26.9.16	-	D.D.R. inspected 10 Remounts received 24th inst. 3 to go to Remount Section for exchange. One to Remounts base.	
"	27.9.16	-	Inspection. H.A. 17th Corps. 1/1st Essex Battery. Visited D. 303 Brigade. R.F.A.	
"	28.9.16	-	Inspection H.A. 17th Corps. 116th Battery.	
"	29.9.16	-	Inspection H.A. 17th Corps 145th Battery.	
"	30.9.16	-	Visited No 5 Hospital, Abbeville, and accompanied O.C. round hospital and horse depôt.	

H.M. Lane 17.50
A.D.V.S.
60TH DIVISION.

Vol 5

War Diary

of A.D.V.S. 60TH DIVISION

October 1916.

October 1916.

WAR DIARY
or
INTELLIGENCE SUMMARY
(Erase heading not required.)

Army Form C. 2118.

Place	Date	Hour	Summary of Events and Information	Remarks and references to Appendices
HERMAVILLE	2.10.16	-	With V.O.'s went round Infantry Transport.	
"	3.10.16	-	Brig-General PECK, A.Q.M.G. 17TH CORPS, inspected Mobile Veterinary Section lines.	
"	5.10.16	-	D.D.V.S. 1ST ARMY, inspected H.A. 17TH CORPS.	
"	6.10.16	-	D.D.R. 1ST ARMY called and looked at horses M.V.S., and reported that 18 out of the last batch of 53 Remounts were nailed and must be evacuated. Inspected 301 Brigade R.F.A. - evacuated 5 Veterinary cases.	
"	7.10.16		Visited M.V.S.	

H.T.Keene H?P?C
A.D.V.S.
60TH DIVISION.

October 1916 (Cont.)

WAR DIARY
or
INTELLIGENCE SUMMARY
(Erase heading not required.)

Army Form C. 2118.

Place	Date	Hour	Summary of Events and Information	Remarks and references to Appendices
HERMAVILLE	8.10.16	—	Headquarters 1st ARMY - Conference D.D.V.S.	
"	9.10.16	—	M.V.S. issued horses R.F.A. LARASSET, and inspected old and prepared lines Pioneer Battalion.	
"	10.10.16	—	303rd Brigade R.F.A. ACQ. 5 horses evacuated for Veterinary reasons, 1 for VICE.	
"	11.10.16	—	Proceeded on 7 days leave to ENGLAND.	
"	13.10.16	—	40 Remounts arrived - fairly good lot - old seasoned animals mostly	

H.J. Mowerouse

A.D.V.S.
60TH DIVISION.

Army Form C. 2118.

WAR DIARY
or
INTELLIGENCE SUMMARY
(Erase heading not required.)

Instructions regarding War Diaries and Intelligence Summaries are contained in F. S. Regs., Part II. and the Staff Manual respectively. Title Pages will be prepared in manuscript.

Place	Date	Hour	Summary of Events and Information	Remarks and references to Appendices
HERMAVILLE.	18.10.16		Returned from leave.	
"	19.10.16		M.V. Section.	
"	20.10.16		302nd Brigade R.F.A. 18 horses evacuated including 4 for VICE.	
"	21.10.16		M.V. Section.	

A.H. Raven Colonel
A.D.V.S.
60TH DIVISION.

WARY DIARY
or
INTELLIGENCE SUMMARY

(Erase heading not required.)

Army Form C. 2118.

Instructions regarding War Diaries and Intelligence Summaries are contained in F. S. Regs., Part II. and the Staff Manual respectively. Title Pages will be prepared in manuscript.

Place	Date	Hour	Summary of Events and Information	Remarks and references to Appendices
HERMAVILLE	22.10.16	-	D.D.R and D.D.V.S. came to office and M.V. Scotson. Inspected 51g R. Howitzer Battery. Horses generally not a good lot - common and many too light. 75% not in good condition. 4 serious cases of Ringworm.	
"	23.10.16	-	Inspected D.A.C. All four sections animals looking well, only EIGHT for evacuation.	
"	24.10.16	-	40 Remounts arrived 9 p.m. R.A. horses good. Chargers and other L.D. horses poor Class and all.	
"	25.10.16	-	11 a.m. M.V.S. 4.30 p.m. Saw Capt Hill arr. in presence of Capt Archer.	
HOUVIN-HOUVIGNEUL	26.10.16	-	Headquarters Division moved to HOUVIN - HOUVIGNEUL.	
"	27.10.16	-	Animals standing the trek very well, except a few H.D. horses Div. Train.	
FROHEN-LE-GRAND	28.10.16	-	To FROHEN-LE-GRAND.	

A.D.V.S.
60TH DIVISION.

Army Form C. 2118.

WAR DIARY
or
INTELLIGENCE SUMMARY

(Erase heading not required.)

Place	Date	Hour	Summary of Events and Information	Remarks and references to Appendices
BERNAVILLE	29/10/16		To BERNAVILLE. Animals on the whole standing the work well.	
"	30/10/16		M.Y. Scoton.	
"	31/10/16		Inspected 181st Brigade - 21st, 22nd and 23rd Battalions and 6th Field Ambulance. All very good except 22nd, the horses of which have fallen away in condition - chiefly owing to change in Transport Officer three weeks ago, and Transport Sergeant evacuated sick. Reported to D.E.	

A.H.eeen
Lt Col
A.D.V.S.
60TH DIVISION.

Vol 6

War Diary.

November 1916.

November 1916.

Army Form C. 2118.

WAR DIARY
or
INTELLIGENCE SUMMARY

(Erase heading not required.)

Instructions regarding War Diaries and Intelligence Summaries are contained in F. S. Regs., Part II. and the Staff Manual respectively. Title Pages will be prepared in manuscript.

Place	Date	Hour	Summary of Events and Information	Remarks and references to Appendices
BERNAVILLE	1.11.16	—	Inspected 18th & 19th Battns & 180th M.G. Coy. All good.	
"	3.11.16	—	Moved to Ailly Le Haut Clocher.	

T.J.M.H. Capt
for A.D.V.S.

A.D.V.S.
60TH DIVISION

Army Form C. 2118.

WAR DIARY
or
INTELLIGENCE SUMMARY
(Erase heading not required.)

Place	Date	Hour	Summary of Events and Information	Remarks and references to Appendices
AILLY LE HAUT CLOCHER.	7.11.16	-	Mallein Testing D.A.C. all animals – Riding horses D.H.Q., Divn! Train, & Signal Coy R.E.	
"	8.11.16	-	Superintended exchange L.D. horses for mules at No 2. Coy. A.S.C. BELLANCOURT.	
"	10.11.16	-	" " " " 3 " " FAMECHON.	
"	11.11.16	-	Mallein Testing 179 Inf Bde, No 2. Coy D.T. 4th F. Amb, 3. Field Coys R.E. Riders & Mules.	

Capt A.V.C.
for Lt Col
A.D.V.S.
60TH DIVISION.

Army Form C. 2118.

WAR DIARY
or
INTELLIGENCE SUMMARY
(Erase heading not required.)

Instructions regarding War Diaries and Intelligence Summaries are contained in F. S. Regs., Part II and the Staff Manual respectively. Title Pages will be prepared in manuscript.

Place	Date	Hour	Summary of Events and Information	Remarks and references to Appendices
AILLY LE HAUT CLOCHER	12.11.16		Mallein Testing 302 Bde R.F.A.	
"	13.11.16		" " 301 " " Lt. Timohey. A.V.C. sent to ABBEVILLE to draw Stores and issue to 179th Inf Bde, R.E, & 4th F. Amb.	
"	14.11.16		Mallein Testing 303 Bde R.F.A. Lt. Timoney A.V.C. takes out Veterinary Stores in car, to 302 Bde. R.F.A. M.V.S. ½ Section entrani LONGPRÉ for MARSEILLES. 2 Veterinary Officers, 7. N.C.Os & 4 men A.V.C. arrived from Base.	
"	15.11.16		Capt. Brett, A.V.C. ½ remaining ½ Section, M.V.S.	
"	16.11.16		Car takes out Veterinary Stores to 301 & 303 Bdes R.F.A. Lt. Heron A.V.C. to MARSEILLES with 3 Sergts A.V.C.	
"	17.11.16		Lt. Moody A.V.C. reports for duty.	
"	18.11.16		Car from D.V.S. ABBEVILLE, brings in Stores in Compliance with telephone request.	

W. Brett Capt. A.V.C.
for A.D.V.S.
A.D.V.S.
60TH DIVISION.

Army Form C. 2118.

WAR DIARY
or
INTELLIGENCE SUMMARY

(Erase heading not required.)

Instructions regarding War Diaries and Intelligence Summaries are contained in F. S. Regs., Part II. and the Staff Manual respectively. Title Pages will be prepared in manuscript.

Place	Date	Hour	Summary of Events and Information	Remarks and references to Appendices
AILLY LE HAUT CLOCHER	20.11.16		Reported to D.V.S. I.G.C. all animals malleined – no reactors.	
LONGPRÉ	24.11.16		Entrained for MARSEILLES.	

T. J/Brett Capt AVC.
for Lt Col.

A.D.V.S.
60TH DIVISION.

Army Form C. 2118.

WAR DIARY
or
INTELLIGENCE SUMMARY

(Erase heading not required.)

Place	Date	Hour	Summary of Events and Information	Remarks and references to Appendices
MARSEILLES	26.11.16		Arrived MARSEILLES.	
"	28.11.16		A considerable number of horses, especially in 302 BDE R.F.A. are suffering from FEVER and PNEUMONIA, the result of train journey. There have been 9 deaths. O/c's Batteries, 302 BDE R.F.A. report that the train was not stopped long enough to water the horses during the 50 hour journey. Two trains had no chance of watering throughout the journey. I consider that the sickness is also due to want of ventilation of the trucks. There are no ventilators in this truck and in many cases the doors were not opened.	
"	30.11.16		Embarked on H.M.T. "IVERNIA".	

Ingthrift Capt. A.V.C.
for R.C.

A.D.V.S.
60TH DIVISION.

www.ingramcontent.com/pod-product-compliance
Lightning Source LLC
Chambersburg PA
CBHW051528190426
43193CB00045BA/2573